Praise For H

For those who don't believe God speaks...
For those who believe God speaks, (just not to me...)
For those who believe God speaks to them, but they've never listened...
For those who have heard God speak (at least I think it was God...)
For those who have heard God speak to them, but didn't know what to do next...

Lynne Lee's book How to Hear God is for you! This book proves, through Scripture, logic and personal experience that God desires to speak to us, that He does speak to us and that we can hear Him and know how to respond. A must read for anyone who desires more intimate communication with their loving, Heavenly Father.

Jeff and Dawn Clark, KingdomCalled.com

Lynne's latest book is filled with solid advice if you desire to hear God's voice. She has compiled years of experience and research into an easy to read, yet fairly comprehensive book that is guaranteed to help you eliminate some of those nagging questions and self-doubts when it comes to accurately hearing God as He leads you through your life.

Jerry Graham, Ph.D., D.Min.

Lynne Lee's How to Hear God contains more than two dozen ways you can discover and tune into the voice of your beloved Creator. Practical and in step-by-step fashion, Lynne addresses key concerns in hearing the voice of God, such as discerning whether a voice is Divine or just you. If you want to enjoy the extravagance of God's heart, hear His wisdom throughout the day, and allow Him to express His abundant life through you, How to Hear

God will guide you along the most adventurous journey of a lifetime.

A small taste of intimacy will whet your appetite for more, and your ability to hear the voice of your lover will increase until His barest whisper captures your heart.

Lisa Rae Preston STEPintoDestiny.com

"How to Hear from God is packed full of practical ways you can hear from God. Lynne has written a comprehensive guide with many valuable insights and step by step instructions on how to hear from God. Her tone is reassuring, encouraging and supportive.

This will be exceptionally valuable for someone beginning to hear from God. However, even if you're experienced at hearing from God, you'll pick up some valuable tips to increase your ability to hear from Him. I'm impressed with how practical and doable Lynne's insights are. Relationship with God is what it's all about and if you want to grow in your ability to hear from God, I recommend you read this book."

Sharon Rose Gibson SharonRoseGibson.com

This book has inspired me to renew my relationship with God. It gives the reader an easy and practical guide of how to hear the voice of God. So many lives will be changed for the better when they read this book. Lynne, you are bringing much needed truths to the Body of Christ with simple words of understanding. This is a must read for every Christian. In the times that we live in now, we all need to hear clearly what God is saying.

Apostle Sharon Billins, SharonBillins.org

How To Hear God

Keys to Hearing God's Voice Every Day

Lynne Lee

CLC Publishing

ChristianLifeCoaching.co.uk

First Printing, March 2014

ISBN-13: 978-1496069580
ISBN-10: 1496069587

Published by CLC Publishing

ChristianLifeCoaching.co.uk

Contents

Introduction

God Wants To Speak
With YOU

G od is a speaking God; He has never stopped speaking to His people. He isn't a mute stone idol. God is continually speaking and He wants YOU to be able to hear Him.

Contrary to popular belief, God isn't just the Author of a set of rules to be obeyed, or a clever philosophy on how to make life a little better. God is a loving Father whose deepest desire is to have a two-way conversational relationship with the apple of His eye, His beloved creation. It thrills me to know that we have an invitation from God Himself into the sacred privilege of a close, intimate relationship with Him.

God not only loves and desires relationship, He *is* relationship. His nature as a triune God clearly demonstrates that He is constantly involved in relationship – Father, Son and Holy Spirit in perfect, constant communication with each other.

It amazes me that God actually wants to speak with us. The God who created the universe, The Almighty; All Powerful God, wants to communicate with His people.

Liberally scattered throughout the whole scriptural account from Genesis to Revelation are the words, "and God said." On many occasions Jesus said, "He who has ears, to hear, let him hear." This clearly indicates the importance Jesus put on hearing God.

The problem is not that God does not speak to us; we have already established that He is speaking all the time. The main hurdle in developing an on-going relationship with God is learning how to recognize His voice.

A helpful way to illustrate how God can be speaking all of the time and for people to be unaware, is to consider how radio receivers work. Transmitting stations are always broadcasting; the radio waves are packed with information that cannot be heard until you have a receiver correctly tuned to the precise frequency.

The aim of this coaching guide is to help you to tune in to the right frequency so that you *can* hear God. Once you discover how to tune in to God's frequency, the next step is to clean up the reception so that you can hear clearly.

When you follow the steps in this guide and regularly put them into practice, you will begin to hear God more often and become confident in hearing God's voice for yourself and for others.

Hearing God is not just for a chosen few

Being able to hear God changes you forever. The personal transformation that can occur in your life as a result of following these simple steps and regularly communing with God is immeasurable.

As you put the words of Jesus into practice within the safe boundaries of a genuine and scripturally sound discipleship relationship with Him, you will discover that hearing God is not just for a super spiritual chosen few. You will find that hearing God for yourself is not as difficult as you might think, and that it is a privilege open to *everyone*, including you. Most important of all you will know that God is communicating with *you* personally and that you *do* hear Him.

Andrew Murray describes prayer as fellowship with the unseen and Most Holy One. Once you have discovered how to tune in to God's voice and learned how to recognize when He is speaking, and what He is saying, you will be equipped to develop a lifestyle of intimate conversation with Him – prayer without ceasing – day long conversations with God.

To develop a culture of hearing God in your life you will need to meet a few simple requirements. They are to:

- Eagerly desire to hear God speaking.
- Devote time to developing your relationship with Him.
- Expect God to speak to you.
- Be receptive to what He says to you.
- Be willing to lay down your own agenda.
- Act on what He says.

Hearing God's voice is not hard, and it is not a privilege reserved for super spiritual people, or a specially chosen few. God wants *you* to hear His voice.

Hearing God can be as natural as having a conversation with your best friend. You *can* hear God each day in the normal moments of everyday life, that is how God intended normal life to be.

I recommend that you keep a journal and record your journey with God. Value what God says enough to record it, and you will soon discover that God really is speaking to you all of the time, and that He is speaking in many different ways.

Whether you are looking to hear God for the first time; or whether you already hear God to a measure, the steps in this coaching guide will help you to hear Him more clearly. Some of you will begin to realize that you have been hearing God much more than you knew, you simply did not recognize that it was God speaking to you.

You will discover that you hear God much more easily when you learn how to *deliberately listen* for His voice. Take a few moments to think about what life would be like if you started to intentionally tune into God's voice and if God Himself taught you how to hear Him. Jesus said,

The Father who sent me is in charge. He draws people to me—that's the only way you'll ever come. Only then do I do my work, putting people together, setting them on their feet, ready for the End. This is what the prophets meant when they wrote, 'And then

they will all be personally taught by God.' Anyone who has spent any time at all listening to the Father, really listening and therefore learning, comes to me to be taught personally. John 6:44-45

Jesus clearly tells us that the only way people can come to Him is if the Father draws them. He goes on to say that the prophets state that God will *personally* teach all those He draws.

Anyone who spends time listening to the Father and learning from Him comes to Jesus to be taught personally – they get to see it with their own eyes, and hear it with their own ears, from Jesus, who directly hears from the Father. He says that to see Him is to have seen the Father.

There is no formula for hearing God, communication with Him comes from simply spending time with Him. How well you hear God will depend on how willing you are to sow into your relationship with Him.

The key to hearing God is building your relationship with Him so that you develop a natural spontaneous flow of communication between you and your Heavenly Father.

My goal in writing this coaching guide is to encourage and inspire you to believe that you can hear God's voice, and to help you to see that you already hear God's voice much more than you think.

My aim is to shatter the myth that only very spiritual people hear God, and help you to see that

God does not just speak through the Bible, or through Prophets, or in an audible voice.

My hope is that you will be encouraged to believe that *you* can hear God, and that you will begin to experience the joy of having two-way communication with your Heavenly Father. God created you because He wants to have fellowship with you. You were made for relationship with God, created to know Him, and have unbroken communion with Him.

My prayer is that you will grow in your capacity to know and understand who God is, and who you are in Him; that you will grow in faith, and discover how to walk with God as Enoch did.

Life as God intended is all about intimacy with God. If you want to live a successful life you need to do *everything* with that in mind. If you do not, you will find yourself burnt out and trying to live your life on an empty tank. *Nothing* in life is as important as your relationship with God.

I invite you to join me on a thrilling journey into the very heart of God.

Chapter 1

Are You Too Busy To Hear God?

Are you too busy DOING to hear what God is saying to you? God wants you to BE before you DO. He wants you to put Him first, spend time rediscovering the art of listening, and have the courage to do what He is doing, and say what He is saying.

God told Israel not to put up permanent dwellings during their journey in the wilderness because they were simply passing through. He wanted His people to be ready to follow the cloud of His presence each time it moved.

When your life is cluttered with obligations and things of the world, they weigh you down and get in the way of your ability to respond to God. In the hurry and busyness of everyday life, you often do not notice God's voice, yet God is speaking all the time and He wants you to hear Him.

What if you could hear from God . . . often?
What difference would that make to your life?

You have a choice, you can either go through life

under your own steam doing your best to work out the right things to do and make good choices, or you can walk with God and benefit from His input and guidance. You can actually have conversations with God just like you do with a friend. Really!

Before you go any further
I have a treat for you!

My prayer is that this short, yet power-packed coaching guide will give you insights and strategies to help you develop your relationship with God the Father, recognize His voice more easily, and hear Him more clearly, so that you can live life as He always intended it to be lived, walking with Him daily.

If you want to go even deeper and would like help on your journey, I'd like to offer you access to free online tutorials and extra helps at:

www.HowToHearGod.co/resources

My gift to you. Be blessed.

Chapter 2

Have You Been Looking
In The Wrong Place?

God not far away, He is very near. Please stop focusing on a far-off God. The miracle of the gospel is that God is with you. He lives within you. God is close, He is part of you, and you are part of Him.

Or didn't you realize that your body is a sacred place, the place of the Holy Spirit? Don't you see that you can't live however you please, squandering what God paid such a high price for? God owns the whole works. So let people see God in and through your body. 1Cor 6:19

You can have natural conversations with God who lives in your heart. Some of the inklings, the slight understandings, and vague ideas that you repeatedly dismiss are actually God speaking to you. God, the Holy Spirit, lives in you; you cannot help but hear Him!

I invite you to rethink your life and choose to agree with what God says in His word even if what you read does not yet seem to be a reality for you. Be encouraged to reorder your priorities, set time aside, and make room for an ever-increasing conscious connection with God.

God says, "Put your relationship with me first." I hope that your response will be to lay aside many of the things that have kept you busy and give the Lord first place in your life.

God doesn't want you to do more FOR Him,
He wants you to spend more time WITH Him

Jesus says, *"I am the Vine, you are the branches.*
When you're joined with Me and I with you, the
relation intimate and organic, the harvest is sure to
be abundant. Separated, you can't produce a thing."
John 15:5

Your Heavenly Father wants you to *choose* to be with Him more of the time. He longs for you to spend more of your day with Him. I strongly encourage you to become closely connected, and then stay closely connected.

Remember that without God you can do nothing of any lasting value. If you really want to grow in God, then you can no longer settle for giving Him second or third or fourth place. I implore you to make friendship with God your first priority.

What will you begin to do differently to make sure
that God gets His rightful place in your life?

Stop and think about that for a few moments and write down your answer in your journal.

I ask the God of our Master, Jesus Christ, the God of glory—to make you intelligent and discerning in knowing Him personally, your eyes focused and clear, so that you can see exactly what it is He is calling you to do, grasp the immensity of this glorious way of life He has for His followers, oh, the utter extravagance of His work in us who trust Him— endless energy, boundless strength! Eph 1: 17-19

My prayer for you is that the God of glory will draw you ever closer to Himself so that you can get to know Him personally. Also that your spiritual eyes will be wide open, and focused, so that you can see exactly what He is calling you to do. May you be able to understand the true extent of the wonderful way of life your Heavenly Father has planned for His followers, and the utter extravagance of His provision for the people who trust Him.

Chapter 3

Can You Really Know God?

If you are like most of the population your answer to the question, "How well do you know God?" will be, "Not nearly as well as I'd like to." It is sad, but true, that for many people God is not very real, yet God longs to be known. God can be so much more real to you than He is now. You do not have to go through life without really ever knowing God.

Knowing God is tied in with being aware of His presence. To become more aware of His presence, all you need to do is learn to listen to the Holy Spirit's promptings and actually begin to use your God-given spiritual senses. You can develop your spiritual senses simply by discovering how to use them and then exercising them regularly.

Most people know that the spiritual world exists, but because they do not have much experience of it, the spiritual realm is not as real to them as the physical world.

There is now a spiritual kingdom all around you waiting for you to recognize it. The spiritual realm is just as real as the physical realm, and with practice you can become more and more aware of it and be at home there.

Belief in the existence of an invisible realm lies at the heart of your walk with God. You enter into the things of God by faith. To have faith is to be sure of the things you hope for and certain of the things you cannot yet see.

To grow in God and the things of the Spirit you need to move your attention from the seen to the unseen. If you really want to follow God, get to know Him better, and hear His voice more clearly, you need to become more spiritually minded and stop separating the physical and the spiritual in your thinking.

A.W. Tozer said, *"We must avoid the common fault of pushing the 'other world' into the future. It is not future, but present. It parallels our familiar physical world, and the doors between the two worlds are open."*

Your spiritual eyes and ears may be weak because you have not used them much but it does not have to stay that way. You can train yourself to use them. You are *in* Christ, Christ lives in you, and with the Holy Spirit's help you can have eyes that see and ears that hear.

As you focus more on developing your relationship with God, you *will* begin to see the things of the Spirit and you *will* begin to hear God more clearly.

May the Lord enable you to see through His eyes and help you to become more and more aware of His presence. May He make Himself known to you in a very real way, and may you become as at home in the spiritual realm as you are in this earthly realm. May the Lord help you to live more and more through the power of His Holy Spirit. May you have continual fellowship with God, hear His voice more and more clearly, and know the joy of day long conversations with Him.

Chapter 4

How Close To God
Do You Want To Be?

Jesus promises that if you seek Him, you *will* find Him. He does not make promises He does not keep!

- How much of your time and energy do you spend seeking the Lord?
- How much time do you spend seeking after other things?

When you take time to consider these questions and answer them honestly, it will help you to see where your priorities actually lie and where your heart really is. Jesus promises that when you seek Him and His Kingdom first, everything else will be added to you. Your life will work so much better when you put Jesus first.

Getting closer to God is the most important thing you can do!

When you were born again you became God's dwelling place. God does not just walk with you, as

He did with Adam in the garden, or as He walked with Enoch. He lives within you.

Stop and think about that for a few minutes. What difference would it make if you lived as though it were true?

You are called to have intimate fellowship with your Heavenly Father, to walk with Him as Jesus did. You are called to be more like Jesus and do the works that He did, Jesus is being formed in you.

The more you fellowship with Him, the more you become aware of His presence and grow to be like Him. God does not have any favourites. Ask Him for an increasing awareness of His presence and dare to believe that He will give you what you ask for.

Develop spiritual awareness until it is as natural as breathing

- Consciously turn your heart towards God.
- Give yourself over to Godliness.
- Spend time developing spiritual receptivity.
- Exercise your faith muscles.

Remember that your Father is always with you because He dwells in you. Continually living in God's presence is His gift to you. You live in the world but you are not of the world, because you are part of God's Kingdom.

How do you develop spiritual awareness?

- Intentionally focus your attention on God at intervals throughout the day and simply thank Him.
- Feed and encourage your soul with thoughts of God, and remind yourself that He is always with you; that there is never a moment when He is not there.
- Practice being heavenly-minded. Make a point of becoming consciously aware of God's presence at set times during the day.
- Talk with your Father through the day, listen for His voice and focus your attention on Him.

Maybe now would be a good time to pray...

Dear Lord, I repent of being so preoccupied with earthly things. You have been here with me all the time, and I haven't been aware of it. Please open my spiritual eyes and help me to become more aware of You, and of Your presence in and around me.

Chapter 5

How To Hear God
More Clearly

Y ou are the living temple of the Holy Spirit. I hope you're beginning to understand that and believe that God lives in you!

If you only look at us, you might well miss the brightness. We carry this precious Message around in the unadorned clay pots of our ordinary lives. That's to prevent anyone from confusing God's incomparable power with us. As it is, there's not much chance of that. 2 Cor 4:7-8

Jesus said, *I am the Vine, you are the branches. When you're joined with Me and I with you, the relation intimate and organic, the harvest is sure to be abundant. Separated, you can't produce a thing. John 15:5*

Please stop trying so hard to be more spiritual, instead *be* who you are. In John 7:38 it says that when you believe in Jesus, springs of living water will flow from your innermost being. That is the Holy

Spirit living within you, expressing His life through you.

You no longer live but Christ lives in you

Jesus lives His life through you just as much as you allow Him to. You do not need to perform, simply give the Holy Spirit permission to work within you, transforming you into who you already are in Christ.

Trying to keep the rules and working hard to please God does not work. You are not under the law; it is Christ's life in you that enables you to live a life that is pleasing to God.

I have been crucified with Christ. My ego is no longer central. It is no longer important that I appear righteous before you or have your good opinion, and I am no longer driven to impress God. Christ lives in me. The life you see me living is not "mine," but it is lived by faith in the Son of God, who loved me and gave Himself for me. Galatians 2:20

You have been crucified with Christ and you are clothed in His righteousness. Stop trying to impress God. *Christ lives in you.* The life you live is not yours, it is lived by faith in Jesus, the Son of God, who loved you and gave Himself for you.

You are called to live a life of faith

You can tune into the amazing life within you, break old habits, and allow the Holy Spirit to form new Holy habits that will support the life you want to live. You do that by fixing your eyes on Jesus, seeing in the Spirit and tuning to His voice. Keep watch to see what He will speak to you. Habakkuk said,

"What's God going to say to my questions? I will climb up to my watchtower and stand at my guard post. There I will wait to see what the LORD says." Habakkuk 2:1

In John we are told that Jesus did nothing except what He saw His Father doing, and that He said nothing other than what He heard His Father saying. Allow Jesus to live His life though you. Continually renew your connection with Him throughout the day.

Consciously connect and listen

When you focus, and intentionally connect and listen, hearing God can become almost effortless, as natural as breathing. When you connect to the flow of God's life within you it will make continuous conversation, *prayer without ceasing,* a very real possibility.

Live by the Spirit

In Romans 8 it says that the mind set on the Spirit is life and peace. God is looking for people who will live by the Spirit, set their mind on the things of the Spirit and develop a habit of doing that again and again and again, so that it becomes as natural as breathing.

Live by Faith

Christ lives in you. When you know that and believe it, you can connect spirit to Spirit, living by faith in all situations, knowing that there is nothing too difficult for God who dwells in you. The key is to believe that you live in Emmanuel (God with us) and that He lives in you. Scripture says that in Him you live and move and have your being. Do you really believe it? The Psalmist said,

I'm an open book to you; even from a distance, you know what I'm thinking. You know when I leave and when I get back; I'm never out of your sight. You know everything I'm going to say before I start the first sentence. I look behind me and you're there, then up ahead and you're there, too—your reassuring presence, coming and going. Psalm 139:2-4

God knows your thoughts even when you are far away from Him. He sees you when you are travelling, when you are at work, and when you are at home. He knows *everything* you do. He knows what you are going to say before you even say it. Nothing is ever a surprise to Him.

Prepare the way for hearing God clearly

I encourage you to decide right now that you will make spending time with God a priority. Make a list of all your priorities and decide what your main priorities will be. What you prioritize will determine how you spend your time.

Are you ready to make time for becoming more conscious of God's presence a priority in your life?

- Ask God to increase your hunger for conscious awareness of His presence.
- Ask Him to show you where you are making compromises and deal with any areas of compromise and sin that might be getting in the way of hearing God.
- Schedule time each day to wait in God's presence. Decide to stop making excuses and choose to spend time in the secret place with God.
- Spend time meditating on His word.
- Invite the Holy Spirit into your everyday life. Ask Him to teach you and guide you.

You *can* walk with God and share His thoughts. You can live in the reality of His presence every day. That is how God intended for it to be.

Are you wondering whether you need to become a better person first?

The only thing that will make you a better person is intimacy with God. You will find that you automatically become a better person as you grow closer and closer to God.

Once you realize who God is and who you are in

relationship to Him, all that is yours in the Kingdom will open to you, and you will begin to walk in your calling and destiny. And as you do that you will become a better person too. That is the way God does things, you do not become a better person by trying harder.

I invite you to stop and think about that for a few moments.

Chapter 6

God Is Always With You

Psalm 139 tells you that God's eyes are always on you, that His thoughts are always directed towards you, and that He is always with you. The Bible also says that God's angels watch over you, *all the time*. That means that you are *never* alone. You may not always be aware of it or believe it, but that does not mean that it is not true. When Jesus said that He would always be with you, He meant it. He said that He would never leave you or forsake you. Never!

If God is truth and speaks only truth that means that Jesus is with you all the time and that the angels really do watch over you. Stop and think about that for a while. What difference would it make to your life if you really believed it and lived as though it were true?

Living in God's continual presence is His gift to you. He is waiting for you to recognise His presence with you. God wants you to stop long enough to have dialogues with Him. He is waiting for you to be aware of His presence and initiate conversations with Him. Do you know that you can talk with God *anywhere?*

Tips to help you become more aware of God's presence

- Practice being more spiritually minded.
- Deliberately focus your attention on God at different times through the day.
- Feed and nourish your soul with thoughts of God as you go through your day.

Talk with your Heavenly Father during the course of the day and make Him your main focus. If you have been blind to His presence up to now, ask Him to open your spiritual eyes and help you to be more aware of His presence in and around you.

When I walk by the wayside, He is with me. When I enter into company amid all of my forgetfulness of Him, He never forgets me. In the silent watches of the night, when my eyelids are closed and my spirit has sunk into unconsciousness, the observant eye of Him who never slumbers is upon me. Thomas Chalmers

Remember that your Father is *always* with you. The more time you spend with Him, the more easily you will become aware of His presence.

Can I really know God and have conversations with Him?

Yes you can. Do not disqualify yourself. God knows all about you and yet He loves you. God knows you inside out. There is nothing that He does not know about you. There are no secrets with God; everything is already out in the open. You cannot surprise Him with anything.

God does not have favourites; He wants *you* to know Him better. Ask Him to give you an increasing awareness of His presence. He will.

Sit at His feet, listen to what He has to say, and then do what He tells you to do. You will save yourself a lot of grief when you take time to listen for His direction and only move into action when you have heard from the all-knowing One.

God says, *"Call to me and I will answer you. I'll tell you marvelous and wondrous things that you could never figure out on your own." Jeremiah 33:3*

God really is expecting you to ask Him questions, and He clearly says that when you do, *He will answer you* and tell you things you do not know. Human striving and zeal will not get you what you want, sitting at His feet and waiting for Him is the key.

God is looking for people who long for intimacy and fellowship with Him and are willing and eager to spend time with Him. As you grow the habit of talking with God about everything, and allow Him in from the first moment of each day, your life will be transformed.

What are you willing to let go of, or do less of, to make room for walking more closely with the Lord?

What changes are you prepared to make to support you in getting the life you want, rather than the one you're used to leading?

How can you create an environment that supports your desire to hear God and walk more closely with Him?

Chapter 7

Can You Really Learn How To Hear God?

You can know God as certainly as you know that you are living and breathing. You can know God as surely as you know things in this physical world.

You become familiar with things in the physical world through your physical senses. Did you know that *you have spiritual senses too*? When you discover your spiritual senses and begin to exercise them, you will gradually become more and more aware of the spiritual realm.

All you need to do is to learn to recognise the promptings of the Holy Spirit and actually learn how to use your spiritual senses. The more you use them, the stronger they will become. If you want to grow in the things of God, start to act on your impressions, the little inklings that you get. Actually do something with them.

How do you learn to use your spiritual senses?

Faith is the key. It is faith that enables your spiritual senses to awaken and function. Without faith, you cannot know God, and you cannot grow in the things of the Spirit. To have faith is to be sure of the things you hope for and to be certain of the things you cannot yet see

Most people believe that the visible world is real and doubt the existence of actual spiritual realms. They do not necessarily deny that spiritual realms exist - they just do not think of them as being real, certainly not as real as this earthly realm.

The difficulty is that people are so preoccupied with the world that they can see that they struggle to see the spiritual realm. But that does not mean that spiritual realms are not real.

You simply need God to open your spiritual eyes. Ask the Lord to awaken your spiritual senses, and shift your focus from what you can see to the unseen. If you really want to know God and become more spiritual, you need to become 'other-worldly.'

Follow the advice of AW Tozer, and avoid the common fault of pushing the 'other world' into the future. God's Kingdom is all around you and within you. It is not future, but present. It parallels our familiar physical world, and the doors between the two worlds are wide open.

God always intended that you enter His Spiritual Kingdom while living on earth

Ask Him to open your spiritual eyes so that you can see more clearly. Ask Him to open your spiritual ears so that you can hear Him speaking to you. When you ask in faith, God will answer you.

But even there, if you seek God, your God, you'll be able to find Him if you're serious, looking for Him with your whole heart and soul. Deuteronomy 4:29

Be sure to remember that your life of faith is a response to God's power...God's Spirit and power does it, not your own effort. 1 Corinthians 2:5

That needs saying again. *Your life of faith is a response to God's power. It is not down to how hard you try*, or how well you follow the *rules*. God does not want your faith to depend on the wisdom of men; or what you think you know, He wants it to rest on His power.

Chapter 8

How Can You Know God's Thoughts?

W ho knows what you are thinking and planning except you? Other people only know what you are thinking when you *tell* them. It is the same with God; except that God is willing to share what He is thinking and planning with you!

Who knows what you're thinking and planning except you yourself? The same with God—except that He not only knows what He's thinking, but He lets us in on it. God offers a full report on the gifts of life and salvation that He is giving us. We don't have to rely on the world's guesses and opinions. 1Corinthians 2:11-12

When you become more spiritually aware, you have access to what God's Spirit is doing. Jesus knows what God is doing, and you have the mind of Christ, that means *you* can know God's thoughts too! It is simply a matter of awakening your spirit and learning how to communicate spirit to Spirit.

Spirit can only be known by spirit, God's Spirit and your spirit in open communion. When you are spiritually alive, you have access to God's thoughts.

Isaiah asked, "*Is there anyone who knows God's Spirit, anyone who knows what He is doing?*" That question has been answered: Jesus knows what God is doing, and His Spirit dwells in *you*.

God shares His thoughts with you through Jesus whose Spirit lives in you. The Bible tells you that His sheep know His voice. If you are a follower of Jesus you have the capacity to hear the voice of God in its many and varied forms.

If you want to learn to communicate spirit to Spirit, ask the Holy Spirit to show you how. Quiet yourself in His presence and ask Him to teach you.

A prayer to help you on your way...

Jesus, forgive me for not living as though You live within me, and for forgetting that I have access to the Father's thoughts through You because I have the mind of Christ. Forgive me for neglecting to spend time with You. Forgive me for forgetting to wait and listen for Your Spirit communicating with me.

Help me to get to know You more, and to live each day more and more aware of Your presence. Lord, draw me closer to You, open my spiritual eyes and spiritual ears, and help me to hear Your voice and live life as though what You say is true.

Chapter 9

The Apple Of His Eye

I hope you are convinced that you were created to live in God's presence and have an intimate friendship with Him. God really does want to be your very best friend. In Romans 5:11 it says that we can rejoice in our wonderful new relationship with God because Jesus has made us friends of God.

Jesus said, *I'm no longer calling you servants because servants don't understand what their master is thinking and planning. No, I've named you friends because I've let you in on everything I've heard from the Father. John 15.14-15*

God longs for you to know Him intimately

Starting from scratch, He made the entire human race and made the earth hospitable, with plenty of time and space for living so we could seek after God, and not just grope around in the dark but actually find Him. He doesn't play hide-and-seek with us. He's not remote; He's near. Acts 17:26-27

God expects you to seek Him, and He makes it possible for you to find Him. He does not leave you to grope around in the dark, and He does not play hide and seek. Stop and think about that for a moment.

You become friends with people through sharing your life with them, and you do that through conversation. Friends talk to each other often, and they share the details of their life. Friends share secrets. God will share His secrets with you when you spend time interacting with Him through the day.

It is possible to carry on a continuous conversation with God just as you would with a close friend. You can talk to Him about what you are doing and what you are thinking, ask Him questions, and pause to listen for His responses.

In Thessalonians, God says that He wants you to pray without ceasing, that means communicating with God as you go through your day. It is possible because *God is not far off;* He is with you *all the time.* Ephesians 4 says that God rules everything and is *everywhere* and in everything.

Smith Wigglesworth said that he never prayed for longer than 5 minutes but never went 5 minutes without praying. Maybe that is something you could aim to move closer towards.

Like many of the spiritual giants, you can know your Heavenly Father far better than you do now. He is waiting to make Himself known to you. All you need to do is to stop long enough to wait and listen, and train yourself to become accustomed to His voice so that you recognize when He is speaking to you.

You can be as close to God as you want to be

God said to the captives in Babylon, *When you come looking for me, you'll find me. Yes, when you get serious about finding me and want it more than anything else, I'll make sure you won't be disappointed.* Jeremiah 29:13

And that is God's promise to you. Keep on asking; keep on seeking until you get what you long for. When you draw close to God, He *will* draw close to you, you will find Him.

To know Jesus as your friend is the greatest privilege you have; not just knowing *about* Him, but really knowing Him. Jesus told the disciples that He would be their friend. They talked with Him about everything and He talked with them daily.

Jesus wants the same level of friendship with you today

It is never too late to start cultivating and nurturing your friendship with God. Talk to Him and meditate on what He says to you. Speak to God and wait for Him to speak to you.

Pray remember what I have recommended to you, which is, to think often on God, by day, by night, in your business, and even in your diversions. He is always near you and with you; leave Him not alone. You would think it rude to leave a friend alone, who came to visit you: why then must God be neglected?

Do not then forget Him, but think on Him often, adore Him continually; live and die with Him; this is the glorious employment of a Christian; in a word, this is our profession, if we do not know it we must learn it. Brother Lawrence

Andrew Murray, in his book 'Waiting on God', writes,

We must not only think of our waiting upon God, but also of what is more wonderful still, of God's waiting upon us. The vision of Him waiting on us will give new impulse and inspiration to our waiting upon Him.

It will give us an unspeakable confidence that our waiting cannot be in vain. If He waits for us, then we may be sure that we are more than welcome, and that He rejoices to find those He has been seeking for.

You are on God's mind all the time
He is always thinking about you

And He wants to be included in everything you do. You can easily include God by talking to Him as you go through your day, and inviting Him to be part of everything. When you do that, you will find that everything you do can be 'spending time' in His presence if you remain aware of Him there with you.

God is with you all the time

Once you get hold of the fact that God is with you all the time you can be in constant communion with Him. Like Brother Lawrence, you can learn to practice the presence of God and be more and more aware of your friend and your Father through the day. You can train yourself to remember that God is always with you and wants to be part of all you do.

Make a point of speaking with God constantly through the day. Talk to Him about everything, share your thoughts with Him and listen for His replies.

Ask yourself what you can do to remind yourself to think about God more and talk to Him more constantly. Whatever it is, plan to do it.

Growing friendship with God is a choice

Ask yourself,

- "How much do I want friendship with God?"
- "Do I want to know God badly enough to develop new spiritual habits?"

- "What will be the cost of not developing my relationship with God?

What could be more important than developing your friendship with God?

What will you do to make sure you grow closer to Him? Take time to stop and think about that now.

What one thing will you begin doing today to ensure that your friendship with God grows?

Write it down where you will see it, and make sure you actually do it. He is worth it!

Chapter 10

Is That You Lord?

How do you know when it is God speaking rather than your own thoughts? This is a very common question. God says He will teach you how to know and recognise His voice when you ask Him to help you. As you grow in your relationship with God, you will become more aware of when it is God speaking and when it is simply your own thoughts. The more you communicate with God, the more familiar His voice will become.

It is easy to confuse your own desires with God speaking to you, especially when something is really important to you. One of the ways of turning down the volume of your own voice is by laying down your own agenda.

When your thoughts or other people's opinions do not line up with God's word you need to dismiss them. The enemy is always looking for ways to confuse you and take you off course, and he will try to do that in any way that he can.

The Bible tells you to resist the enemy. How do you do that? You can silence the enemy by speaking the word of God as Jesus did.

Here's another clue as to whether it is God's

voice rather than your own thoughts – if it is God's voice, it will lead to peace.

Learning to recognise God's voice is a process

Remember, as a believer and follower of God, you have the Holy Spirit living within you. If you ask Him, He will help you to discern when it is the Father's voice you are hearing.

When you renew your mind with God's written word and spend time in His presence, you have the mind of Christ. The more time you spend renewing your mind with God's word, the easier it is to discern when it is God speaking rather than your own thoughts and ideas.

Jesus said, *"My sheep recognize My voice. I know them, and they follow Me." John 10:27*

The Friend, the Holy Spirit whom the Father will send at my request, will make everything plain to you. He will remind you of all the things I have told you. John 14:26

You are one of His sheep and *you can* hear God's voice. Because you belong to God and follow His ways you can be confident that you will be able to recognise the voice of your Lord and your Heavenly Father.

It takes a bit of effort, but you can train yourself to recognise when it is God speaking. You learn by practicing and being prepared to make mistakes.

Please do not let fear of making a mistake stop you from stepping out in faith. God is a loving Father and He will take care of your honest mistakes.

The more you stop and spend time listening for God, the easier it will be to distinguish between the different voices.

The key is to evaluate what you hear in the light of God's word

Trust God from the bottom of your heart; don't try to figure out everything on your own. Listen for God's voice in everything you do, everywhere you go; He's the one Who will keep you on track. Don't assume that you know it all. Run to God! Run from evil! Proverbs 3:5-7

Sometimes you will struggle to hear God about something that is important to you, or you will not hear as clearly as you would like. At other times, you will think you have heard God and respond to what you have heard only to find that you made a mistake.

When that happens, ask the Lord to help you see where you got it wrong, *learn from your mistakes, and do not let them hold you back* from stepping out in faith the next time. God will teach you through your mistakes, and it is so much better to give yourself permission to make mistakes than never to step out in faith.

The problem for most people is that they have been living without hearing God for such a long time that they do not realise that it is not normal to go through life without hearing God.

Normal is hearing from God EVERY day

Is that your expectation? Are you actually scheduling time to spend exclusively with God every day? Or are you just trying to squeeze Him in around everything else you do?

Are you still struggling to believe that God will speak to you and that you will be able to hear Him?

Confess your lack of faith to God. Ask Him to increase your faith and dare to believe that He will. Have the courage to exercise your faith muscles so that you can grow stronger in the things of God. Decide now that you will overcome your doubts and keep on knocking.

It is worth taking time to train yourself to recognise God's voice. He has the words of life and He wants to direct your paths. Stop and listen to God, and be prepared to do whatever it takes to learn how to hear Him more clearly. He is worth it and the rewards are great!

Chapter 11

Wrong Thinking That Disrupts Your Hearing

When you want to hear God but you do not seem to be able to hear Him no matter you do, it is time to do a little soul searching. When you do that, you will probably discover thoughts or beliefs that are getting in the way. Thoughts such as:

- I don't deserve to hear God.
- I'm not worthy.
- I'm not spiritual enough.

God still speaks to you even when you do not deserve to hear Him

Now that we know what we have—Jesus, this great High Priest with ready access to God—let's not let it slip through our fingers. We don't have a priest who is out of touch with our reality. He's been through weakness and testing, experienced it all—all but the sin. So let's walk right up to Him and get what He is so ready to give. Take the mercy, accept the help. Hebrews 4:14-16

You can approach God with boldness and confidence even when you do not feel deserving, or worthy, or spiritual enough!

What the Bible says about faith

Faith is being sure of what you hope for and certain of what you do not see. Faith means *being sure of* the things you hope for and *knowing that something is real even if you do not see it.* Hebrews 11:1

When you ask, believe and do not doubt

Ask boldly, believingly, without a second thought. People who "worry their prayers" are like wind-whipped waves. Don't think you're going to get anything from the Master that way, adrift at sea, keeping all your options open. James 1:6

Faith is a choice; faith is a decision to believe whether or not there is any physical evidence to support your belief.

There is not much point hoping to receive something from God while entertaining doubts that it will happen. When you give in to doubt, it is hard to receive anything from God. Jesus said, *"According to your faith be it unto you."*

If your faith is shaky your doubts will act as a barrier to you hearing God. Even when you have heard God, if you have doubts, you are likely to dismiss what you hear as being your own thoughts or ideas.

As a much loved child of God, it is your birth right to have fellowship with Almighty God, and communicate with Him! He *wants* to converse with you. The door is *always* open.

You can approach God at any time and in any place

But I don't know how to go about having those kinds of conversations with God.

You are not alone! And the good news is that it could work to your advantage because you do not have lots of preconceived ideas getting in the way of hearing what God has to say to you.

When you do not know how to do something, or you are not sure, ask for help

Jesus said, *"Don't bargain with God. Be direct. Ask for what you need. This isn't a cat-and-mouse, hide-and-seek game we're in. If your child asks for bread, do you trick him with sawdust? If he asks for fish, do you scare him with a live snake on his plate? You wouldn't think of such a thing. So don't you think the God who conceived you in love will be even better?" Matthew 7:7-11*

Keep on asking God to help you, and you will receive what you ask for

Do you believe that? Then ask God to help you recognise His voice, choose to believe that you will hear Him, expect to hear, and position yourself to listen.

Chapter 12

God the Creative Communicator

In the book of Job we are told that God does speak, first one way and then another, though we may not pay attention or recognize it. God speaks again and again and again though people are often not aware of it. Job 33:14

God is already speaking to you in ways you often overlook because you do not yet recognise that it is God speaking to you

He has many different ways of speaking and He does not always speak in the way that you expect Him to. Most people hear God through His written word, His peace, a still small voice, circumstances, other Christians, wisdom, and common sense. God speaks in many other ways too. Some of God's ways of speaking may be unfamiliar to you.

Beware of getting bogged down with *how* God speaks. The important thing is to *expect* God to speak and be ready for Him to speak to you in ways that may be unfamiliar to you.

If you want to hear God, you need to tune in to His voice

As I have already mentioned, the more you get to know God and His ways the easier it is to tune in and recognise when it is God speaking. Learning to recognize when God is speaking takes time and effort. The more often you meet with God and talk with Him, the clearer His voice becomes. When you become familiar with God's presence and His voice, it is so much easier to notice when He is speaking to you.

Sometimes you will not hear God because you are not really expecting Him to speak, or because you are expecting Him to speak in a certain way. When God speaks in a way you do not expect, you might miss what He is saying.

God is full of surprises. You need to remind yourself that God is not human, and His ways are not your ways

It is a mistake to limit Him to what you already know or expect. You need to be open to God speaking to you in any way He chooses and not just in ways that you are already at ease with. People hear from God in many different ways and God's voice is not limited to words. He speaks through *all* of His creation.

Many people hear God speaking through circumstances or their physical surroundings. In the Bible, God spoke to people in ways that they could see and experience in their daily lives. God communicated with people through what was obvious and part of their natural environment. He does the same with you today.

There is no formula; there is no set way of hearing God. You can hear Him through all of your senses. The sound of His voice comes in many different ways. I like the way Larry Randolph put it in his book, *Spirit Talk*:

The human body is like a giant ear drum that processes thousands of pieces of information from every spectrum of life.

God often speaks in a combination of ways

God speaks in many different ways, and He often creates a symphony that you only begin to hear and understand once you recognise that God is speaking to you and you know how to tune in to what He is saying.

These are some of the many ways God speaks to you and some of the means He uses to communicate His message:

An inner voice	Your conscience
Inspired thought	God's peace
Impressions	Nature
Dreams	The heavens
Visions	Symbolic language
Visitations	Songs
Wisdom	Coincidences
Mental pictures	Circumstances
Physical senses	His written word
Other people	An audible voice
Prophecy	Events in nature
Fiction	Billboards
Films	An inner knowing

God's word is a lamp to guide your feet and a light for your path. Psalm 119:105

You have probably had experience of Scripture suddenly coming into your mind, or a Bible reference, which, when you look it up, speaks directly to your situation. God often speaks through Scripture. You need to read Scripture, study it, and meditate on it. God's written word is a lamp to your feet and a plumb line to measure everything by.

God our loving Creator first communicated with His creation in the Garden of Eden. And all through Scripture there are many examples of God speaking to man.

People seem to have forgotten that God is a speaking God and that He speaks to His people.

Either that or they think that He does not speak any more, so they do not expect to hear Him. Sadly most people live in an emptiness of spiritual silence, yet God the Creator and loving Father is still speaking today. He never stopped speaking. All you need to do is learn how to tune in and recognize the many facets of the sound of His Voice.

I hope you are encouraged to believe that God is speaking to you. You *can* hear God's voice every day; it is much easier than you think.

Chapter 13

Tuning Into God's Frequency

I f you want to develop your spiritual hearing, one of the first things you need to do is learn to still your mind and stop long enough to listen. Have you ever tried *just* listening? You simply need to sit quietly, not ask anything, and just listen. It is in those still, quiet times that you will begin to sense God the Father's heartbeat.

Listening prayer is a lost art
That can easily be recovered

Listening for God is a bit like tuning in to a radio station, but instead of tuning into a channel on the radio, you are tuning in to God's thoughts. Once you know what God's voice sounds like, it is so much easier to recognise and tune into next time.

- Find a quiet place – even little noises may be distracting, particularly when you are just starting to learn to hear.
- Get into a comfortable position and relax.
- Close your eyes to shut out distractions.

- Wait and listen.
- Wait some more.

God promised to lead you by His Spirit and He said that His sheep will know His voice. You are one of His sheep. *Simply decide to believe what God says and agree with His Word.* Expect Him to lead you by His Holy Spirit and expect to recognise God's voice as you wait.

You could begin by speaking words of faith and praying something like this:

Because I am a believer who follows Jesus, I can and will hear God's voice. Thank you Father that I do know your voice. Thank you that I hear you speaking to me. Thank you that hearing you is becoming a normal part of my everyday life.

Put your faith into action

Open the ears of your heart and start listening for the voice of Holy Spirit. The more you trust that you are hearing God's voice and follow His promptings, the more clearly you will hear Him.

Before long, hearing from God will not be something that happens every now and then, it will be part of your daily life, and become almost as natural as breathing.

What is the Spirit of God telling you today?

Still your mental chatter, tune in, and listen for the voice of God. And be sure to record what you hear and act on it.

Chapter 14

The Secret Place

God *is* speaking all the time. If you follow the steps I outline in this guide and set time aside to practice hearing God, you will find that you can hear God speaking to you more easily, more of the time.

In Psalm 46, God says, *Be still and know that I am God.* Stop striving, let go, relax, and know that He is God. When you shut out the clamour that is such a big part of modern life and take time to be still, it will become easier to draw near to God and hear Him speak in your heart.

You will find it easier to be still if you find a place where you can be alone and will be undisturbed, somewhere away from distractions. Once you find a place where you will not be disturbed, quiet the many voices and thoughts fighting to get your attention. If you have difficulty with this and if your mind is busy, try jotting down the thoughts that come so that you can stop focusing on them and deal with them later.

If you become conscious of sin getting in the way of you hearing, confess your sin so it is no longer a barrier. If your mind continues to be busy, visualise Jesus there with you.

The key is to be so focused on Jesus that everything else fades into the background. When you become still, you will begin to sense God's presence.

By becoming still, I mean doing nothing other than focusing on God so that you can experience His presence. Once you are still, it will be easier to hear God. You may find that spontaneous images begin to come to your mind and you will probably begin to hear God's voice in your heart as spontaneous thoughts.

1. When you enter the secret place, spend the first few minutes becoming still. When you are still, you will begin to sense God.
2. Once you are still and have quieted your thoughts, focus on the Lord.
3. Visualize Him there with you and listen for Him speaking.

The more you practise becoming still, the easier it gets and the more quickly it all comes together.

Many people hear God speak through spontaneous thoughts, a Scripture coming to mind, pictures, feelings, or impressions. He sometimes speaks in an audible voice.

As you have already seen, God speaks in many ways. The way that *you* hear God may not be the same as someone else you know. Different people tend to hear God in different ways. The way that *you* hear God may not be the same as someone else you know.

When God speaks to you, showing you what He wants you to know or pray about, He often does it through spontaneous thoughts that interrupt your own thought process. As you still yourself and wait, spontaneous thoughts will begin to flow and you will find yourself having an inner conversation with God.

Look for the Lord there with you as you wait, and watch Him as He speaks to you

You will find that if you look, you will begin to see. You may start to see spontaneous images in the same way that you hear spontaneous inner thoughts.

You might find that inner vision comes so easily that you want to reject it, thinking that it is just you making it up. Yet if you persevere and record what you see and hear, your doubts will soon give way to faith as you begin to recognise that what you are seeing and hearing is mostly from God.

You will find it helpful to have a journal with you as you wait, and record what you see and hear. Your journal is your way of saying to God, "I value what you say to me." It is also a step of faith, demonstrating that you are expecting God to speak to you.

Write in faith, simply believing that God is speaking to you as you have asked Him to do. Do not censor what you are receiving. Let it flow. You can test it later, making sure that it lines up with

Scripture, and even sharing what you have heard with a trusted friend.

You will be surprised at how much more you begin to hear when you start to journal. You will probably begin to realise that God has been speaking all along and you just did not recognise that it was God speaking to you. Put aside any doubts you might have and trust that God really is present and speaking to you.

When you are ready to wait, look and listen

- Find a quiet place and spend some time in worship.
- Sit quietly and visualize yourself with Jesus.
- Talk to Him and ask Him questions. Listen and sense His reply.
- Write down His answers.

Be like Samuel who said, "Speak for your servant is listening." Afterwards check that what you heard lines up with Scripture and that you have peace with what you believe you have heard.

Chapter 15

Biblical Meditation

Meditation is simply thinking about the things of God. Why do you need to meditate? Because God's word tells you to! What you think about influences your behaviour. That is one of the reasons why God encourages you to think about His Word, or meditate on it.

And don't for a minute let this Book of The Revelation be out of mind. Ponder and meditate on it day and night, making sure you practice everything written in it. Then you'll get where you're going; then you'll succeed. Joshua 1:8

The Bible plainly tells us to delight in God's Word, to meditate on it day and night, to think about it and chew it over.

Thrill to God's Word, you chew on Scripture day and night. You're a tree replanted in Eden, bearing fresh fruit every month, never dropping a leaf, always in blossom. Psalm 1:2-3

God clearly says to keep His word ever in mind and be sure to put it on your lips. Ponder and meditate on it day and night, making sure you *do* what it says. Your prosperity and success depend on it.

Meditation is focused thinking, you simply focus on whatever God leads you to focus on. It might be a verse of Scripture, God's presence, who God is, or many other things. Whatever God leads you to chew over, simply think about it, over and over again. Read His word, think about it, and speak it out.

Christian meditation is a form of contemplative prayer:

- Quieting your mind.
- Focusing on the things of God.
- Becoming more aware of His presence.

All that you need is

- A peaceful place.
- Undisturbed time set aside to be still and do nothing other than know God.

There isn't anything else that will do more to transform your life, renew your mind, and cause you to become more like Jesus, than taking time to ponder and reflect on the Word of God every day.

When you read all the mentions of meditation in the Bible, you will be amazed at the benefits God promises to people who regularly reflect on His written Word.

Among other things, Christian meditation helps you to:

- Maintain peace of mind.
- Overcome negative thoughts.
- Deepen your relationship with God.
- Be more content.

Meditating is a simple way of spending quality time with God and immersing yourself in His teaching. It teaches you to control your thoughts, leads to spiritual insights, and it promotes emotional well-being.

You can best serve God when your heart is quieted and focused on Him. Meditation takes your focus from yourself and this world and refocuses your attention to reflect on God's Word, His nature, His abilities, and His deeds. It leads you to prayerfully ponder, wonder about, and chew over the Scriptures.

When you meditate on Scripture you give the Holy Spirit opportunity to bring the word of God to life, and to activate God's life giving word.

What should you meditate on?

Summing it all up, friends, I'd say you'll do best by filling your minds and meditating on things true, noble, reputable, authentic, compelling, gracious—the best, not the worst; the beautiful, not the ugly; things to praise, not things to curse. Philippians 4:8

You communicate with God spirit to Spirit

The main purpose of Christian meditation is communion with the living God. The most important things in your life are your walk with God and your friendship with Him.

If you want to know God better, rather than just knowing about Him, you need to spend time developing your relationship with Him. The more time you spend with Him, the more you will become like Him. Being more aware of God's presence really will change you from the inside out.

In Psalm 46 it says, "Be still and know that I am God." You will find it easier to connect with God when you still and quiet your soul.

When you first begin to meditate, you will probably find that you are distracted by everyday things. Bring every thought captive, do not focus on the distractions, train yourself to let them go. If you stop being bothered about them, they will begin to fade away.

Meditation will help you to

- Still your mind and become more aware of what you are thinking.
- Become aware of your mental chatter.

Once you are more aware of your internal chatter, you can begin to exchange it for God's thoughts and His words.

Just as you rest your body, you need to rest

your mind. Meditation will help you to detoxify your mind from accumulated mental clutter and find rest and peace in God. When you are still, you will find it easier to tune in to God's thoughts, know His mind, receive His peace, and hear His voice.

Tips for successful meditation

- Find a quiet place and allow plenty of time so that you won't feel pressure to hurry.
- Choose a comfortable place where your body and mind can be relaxed.
- Discipline yourself to set aside regular time to meditate.
- You could start with as little as 15 minutes and gradually increase the time.
- Be prepared to keep at it, persevere and you will break through.

If you have been sensing that there is something missing from your relationship with God, I encourage you to regularly spend time alone with Him, doing nothing else other than paying attention to Him, and spending time with Him.

If you are not meditating regularly, you are missing out on treasure

I hope that you are inspired to start learning how to meditate. It really will help you to draw closer to God, become more and more aware of His presence, and tune in to the sound of His voice.

If you are convinced, and want to introduce regular meditation into your daily routine, I recommend you make time to plan meditation into your schedule now while you are still thinking about it. When will you start?

If you need a little more convincing

In the Old Testament, there are two Hebrew words used for meditation: hāgâ (Hebrew: הגה), which means to sigh, murmur, utter, ponder, or meditate, and sîḥâ (Hebrew: החיש), which means to muse, rehearse in your mind, or contemplate.

Lectio Divina

Christian meditation began with the early Christian Monks who practiced reading the Bible slowly. The monks carefully considered the deeper meaning of each verse of Scripture as they read it. As they meditated on Scripture, the monks found themselves praying spontaneously, and their prayers led to a simple loving focus on God. They called their wordless love for God *contemplation.*

This slow, thoughtful reading of Scripture while pondering its meaning is a spiritual practice called *divine reading.* The progression from Bible reading, to meditation, to prayer, to loving regard for God, became known as *Lectio Divina* – or "holy reading."

Meditation takes practice, but eventually your mind will become still without much effort and you will be glad you persevered. Plan to set time aside and start making meditation part of your daily routine.

Chapter 16

Journaling From Eternity

W hat makes you so desperate to hear God? I think it's a combination of two things: you sense that something is missing from your walk with God, and you hear His call to come aside and spend time with Him.

God longs to talk with you as He did with Adam, and Moses, and Enoch, and Jesus. You can live in friendship and daily communication with God just as they did. You were created for fellowship with God. He longs for continual, open and honest communication with everyone.

John 17:3 says, *And this is real and eternal life: That they know You, The one and only true God, And Jesus Christ, whom you sent.*

Eternal life is knowing God the Father and His Son Jesus

Know, in this passage, means 'to be intimately acquainted with someone in a growing, progressive relationship.' You can live in friendship and daily conversation with God – that is how He always intended it to be. In Proverbs 8:32-36, God says:

So, my dear friends, listen carefully; those who embrace these my ways are most blessed. Mark a life of discipline and live wisely; don't squander your precious life. Blessed the man, blessed the woman, who listens to me, awake and ready for me each morning, alert and responsive as I start my day's work. When you find me, you find life, real life, to say nothing of God's good pleasure. But if you wrong me, you damage your very soul; when you reject me, you're flirting with death.

I encourage you to turn these verses into prayer and ask God to give you listening ears:

The Master, God, has given me a well-taught tongue, So I know how to encourage tired people. He wakes me up in the morning, wakes me up, opens my ears to listen as one ready to take orders. The Master, God, opened my ears, and I didn't go back to sleep, didn't pull the covers back over my head. Isaiah 50:4

How to get started with journaling to hear God

Take your journal and set aside time to be still and pray. Ask the Lord what He wants you to know about yourself. Then write down the quiet thoughts that come to your mind as you wait.

This simple exercise could change your life. It

will help to open your eyes to how much God loves you and what He thinks of you. You matter to God; you are the apple of His eye, His much loved child. When you ask God to tell you what He thinks of you. His answer will mirror Jeremiah 29:11

I have it all planned out— plans to take care of you, not abandon you, plans to give you the future you hope for.

Any thoughts that condemn you or make you feel bad about yourself will not be from God. God may gently convict you but He will not condemn you. There will always be redemption in what God says to you.

You could try asking God what His thoughts are towards someone He has put on your heart. Ask Him for words of encouragement for them and record what God says to you.

Do not censor as you write. Let the thoughts flow. Give the Father an opportunity to say whatever He wants to say to you and prepare to be surprised.

You will find that life works much better when you operate out of spending time with the Father and hearing His heart for you. When I want to know what God has to say to me I often make time to sit undisturbed and write in my journal so I have a record of our conversation.

Today I sense the Father leading me to share two of my journal entries with you. On November 3rd I wrote:

What do you want me to know today Father? I'm here to listen. I love hearing what you have to say to me.

This is what I sensed the Lord say in reply:

I really am Abba, your Daddy. Believe it. You are precious to Me, and what matters to you matters to Me. I love the way you are drawing aside to have special times of communion with Me. Think of how you are with your children and how it gladdens your heart when they choose to spend time with you and ask for your wisdom...

Know that I love you. I will provide all you need and direct your paths. Remember what I said about focus. Focus on one thing and complete it before moving onto the next.

I AM giving you tools and support to help you do what I have called you to do. Be reassured that you are on the path that I have mapped out for you.

It is My idea that you offer How To Hear God's Voice as a coaching program. People are hungry and they are looking for Me, desperate to know how to hear Me. Run with it, have fun with it and listen for My voice in it. I will direct your steps and show you what it looks like.

You have wisdom because you take time to listen. Before you say yes to invitations check to see that it is where I AM working, and have the courage to say no even to good things that will simply keep you busy.

You know more than you know you know. You

hear Me more than you know you do. Many times when you have spontaneously thought to do something it has been My prompting. Have the courage to follow those promptings even when they seem silly to you.

Continue to delight in me. IMMERSE yourself in the things that are dear to My heart and yours and be free to be you. I love you, and so do your family and friends. You don't need to try to be like anyone else, simply be you. Who you are in Me is delightful. You cause My heart to sing and I delight to bless you.

Know that you walk in My blessing and enjoy it. Enjoy what I give you and enjoy who you have become. Delight yourself in abundance and prepare to be surprised at what I will do.

You are being used to transform many lives. Your reach is further than you know.

It's time to CELEBRATE. Celebrate what I have done and who you have become in Me. Celebrate and know that My goodness and loving kindness last forever. Pick up the threads I hand you and I will show you how to weave them into a beautiful tapestry. Don't concern yourself with what it will look like. Simply follow My directions and know that it will be beautiful. I will take care of everything just like good daddies do.

Journaling is such a powerful way to tune into what the Lord is saying, I hope you are encouraged to try this for yourself.

And for added measure, here is part of my November 9th journal entry:

It's a red letter day! No accident that I am writing in red today. It's interesting to note that the Lord is already speaking through events and coincidences. Why is today so significant? Because I am writing a book that will be published. How exciting is that!! It will become a series of books...

It feels like You have brought me back to why I went online in the first place – to help people with the help that helped me. If my excitement is anything to go by, then I am about to walk into my destiny. I need to know whether this is an idol that will get in the way and detract from my true purpose...But enough from me, I want to know what You have to say...

Still and quiet your soul and wait. There's no rush, sit a while with Me and rest. Bask in My presence and let's enjoy one another.

Just as your lounge echoes light and nourishes the soul, restoring peace, so will you. Your mission is to do people good. Your books will give people who can't meet with you one on one an opportunity to benefit from the wisdom I have placed in you.

Your name is no accident – Lynne – by the pool or waterfall, refreshing one. You bring encouragement and refreshment wherever you go. Your books will bring hope and encouragement, they will provide keys. Run with this, it is My doing, it was My idea.

Think on how this began. It was born out of prophecy and vision. What is happening now is the fulfillment of a lifetime of desire and longing. I planted the desire to write. I have riches for you to share and now is the time to release them. These last few years have laid the foundation and infrastructure to make it possible.

Keep on dreaming, dream with Me and dare to do what you once thought to be impossible, nothing is impossible with me. I AM the God of infinite possibilities. Partner with Me and allow My Holy Spirit to lead you and show you the way.

Know that you CAN do what I have called you to do. When I call, I also equip – and you are well-equipped.

Enjoy this time and know that the best is yet to come. Put aside any doubts you have and know that I AM the enabler...I will enable you to do this. I will give you what you need when you need it and I will show you how.

I have already connected you with the people who can help and support and cheer you on. You will see your dreams come into being, and hope fulfilled will be like a tree of life to you.

In the physical realm, winter is fast approaching, but for you, spring is here. The long dormant seeds are bursting forth into life. Enjoy the garden I AM creating for you. Delight in my creation and know that I do all things well.

I hope you can see how powerful journaling can be. When God speaks to me, I take notice and act on what I hear, so I have been busy! This coaching guide is some of the fruit.

If journaling to hear from God is new to you, I encourage you to dive in and try it for yourself.

Chapter 17

A Guide To
Spiritual Journaling

By now it is probably obvious that I am a journaling enthusiast, that is because I know it can be a powerful aid to focusing your attention and helping you to hear God more clearly. I have included two chapters on journaling to help you discover the joys of journaling to hear God's voice, and recording your adventures with Him. As you saw in the previous chapter, journeying through life with God, and recording your interactions in a journal can be a great source of comfort and encouragement.

Journaling is simply a way of recording your time with God. It helps you to pay more attention to Him, and acts as a reminder of what He has said. Your journal is a safe way of learning to hear God and record your responses to what you have heard. By keeping a record, you can easily see what He has been doing, how far you have come, and where you are going.

For me a journal is much more than a place to

record daily events. It is a place to document inner growth and personal discovery. It acts like a mirror. Keeping a journal helps you to understand how God is working in your life.

Your journal is a safe place to explore things with God and can be a working document where you generate and record ideas that result from the time you spend with Him.

Keeping a journal will help to enlarge your vision and increase your expectancy. It will help you to keep you in good spiritual shape and stay true to your values. Your journal can be a safe place to process what God is doing in your life and the lives of those around you.

Journaling leads to personal growth and discovery through writing and reflection. It helps you to see where you are going with God and to understand your spiritual journey. Your journal will provide a record that shows you how far you have journeyed, what God has been doing in your life and how much you have grown.

Your journal can be anything you want it to be

It could be a catalogue of your thoughts and prayers and God's answers. A collection of wisdom and insight gleaned from God's word and from others. A record of encounters with other Christians that God puts across your path...whatever serves you.

Tips for spiritual journaling

Start by praying. Ask the Holy Spirit, your Counsellor and Teacher, to lead you as you journal.

Write what is on your heart. Talk to God; be honest with Him and with yourself. Share your joys, victories, desires, frustrations, uncertainties and heartaches with Him. Write down your goals, prayers, dreams, memories, and special events. Record Biblical and spiritual insights and revelations, and write out your praises to God.

Listen and document. Record what God puts on your heart and what He is saying through your dreams and through other people.

Date every entry. This will help you to see your progress and it makes it much easier to find things when you want to refer to them again.

Highlight Scriptures that God gives you and words that He speaks to your heart, so you can easily find them in your journal when you want to re-read them. Sometimes God speaks the same thing in different ways as He attempts to get your attention and impress on you the importance of what He is saying. A journal helps you to spot that.

Keeping a journal helps you to make sense of your life. It helps you to stop and notice what is happening and what is being said, understand it, and respond. A journal helps you to become aware of the many signs of God's presence that you might otherwise overlook.

There is no right or wrong way to journal!

I recommend that you resist the urge to immediately evaluate what you write. Please do not censor your thoughts. Write freely, allowing your thoughts to flow uninterrupted.

It is a good idea to do a summary every few months. I am always encouraged when I do this, amazed at what God has been saying, and surprised to note how many precious exchanges have already slipped from my memory.

I leave you with a thought...

The unexamined life is not worth living... Socrates

If you would like to start journaling to help you hear God more easily, you will find a link to a really helpful guide in the bonus section.

Chapter 18

The Words Left The Page!

God speaks through His written Word too. The Bible is not just dry words recorded long ago, it is living and active, and God is speaking to you through His written word today.

Hearing God through the Bible

God means what he says. What He says goes. His powerful Word is sharp as a surgeon's scalpel, cutting through everything, whether doubt or defence, laying us open to listen and obey. Hebrews 4:12

You need to read God's word regularly, but please do not *just read it*, study and meditate on it too. It is designed to be a lamp to your feet and a plumb line to test everything by. When you read your Bible, read it thoughtfully and *expect* God to speak to you through its pages.

When you are first learning to hear from God, you will probably find that you hear Him more easily through Scripture. A Bible passage will suddenly come alive to you, it will seem to jump out from the page and you will understand it in a way you did not before.

God will speak to you about things that are not actually in the Bible, but if it is God speaking, what you hear will always agree with the principles you find in His Word. If you hear something that does not agree with what God says in Scripture, you need to reject it as not being from God.

John 6:63 says that the words that Jesus spoke are spirit and life. You need to feed on God's word to be spiritually healthy.

God's word is spiritual food. You need fresh food EVERY day to grow strong in God

Scripture is a guide to train you in God's ways. You need to know what God says about things. If you do not know what the Bible says, you can easily be deceived into believing that what you think or hear is God leading you, when it is not.

There are many ways to read and hear through God's written word. Here are a few ideas to get you started.

1. Read a whole book through at one sitting to get a feel for what God is saying.
2. Read the same book in 5 different versions so that it really becomes a part of you.
3. Take one verse or passage and meditate on it.
4. Use study aids to help you unlock the meaning of what you are reading.

5. Read through the Psalms for months at a time until you come to know them well.
6. Read one chapter of Proverbs a day alongside whatever else you are reading.
7. Personalise what you are reading and pray God's word back to Him.
8. Invite the Holy Spirit to come alongside as you read and allow Him to be your teacher.
9. Do as the early monks did and read the Bible slowly considering the deeper meaning of each verse of Scripture as you read it.

Please do not think that you need to do all of this at once. If what I'm describing is new to you, take one step at a time. If time is limited, take what time you have and use that. Give God the little you have and trust Him to increase it like the loaves and fishes.

I cannot stress enough how important it is to know what the word of God says. Knowing and understanding God's written word will help to keep you from falling into deception as you grow in hearing God.

If you have a dream, a prophecy, a vision, inner thoughts or an audible voice that does not line up with God's word, you can be confident that it is not God speaking to you.

Your Father has given you His written word to help keep you on track

When you read God's word, it renews your mind.

Every Scripture is God-breathed and profitable for teaching, for reproof, for correction, and for instruction in righteousness...2 Timothy 3:16-17

Please beware of falling into the trap of taking words out of context so that they fit with what you want to believe God is saying. When you are learning to hear God it is important to check *everything* out with His written word, and if in doubt, ask for insight from a mature believer who is more familiar with God's ways.

The Bible says many wonderful things about the benefits of knowing Scripture. Psalm 119 has much to say about it, and I recommend that you read that psalm again and again.

Dear friend, listen well to my words; tune your ears to my voice. Keep my message in plain view at all times. Concentrate! Learn it by heart! Those who discover these words live, really live; body and soul, they're bursting with health. Proverbs 4:20-22

As you discover how to hear God in different ways, always remember the importance of God's written word - it will help you to go in the right direction and keep you from being deceived.

Chapter 19

Conscientious Reflector

God also speaks to you through your conscience. By that, I mean an inner voice, or sense, that guides you when you make choices.

God often speaks in a voice that is best described as a still, small voice. It is a voice that everyone is capable of hearing. The biggest problem is learning to distinguish this still small voice of God from all the other voices that are competing for your attention.

How do you know whether the voice you associate with conscience is really God's voice and not simply your own desires, or the voice of flawed families, friends, or teachers?

The voice of your conscience is the voice of Holy Spirit speaking to your human spirit

Jesus said that He would send His Holy Spirit to live in you and be your guide. Part of the Holy Spirit's work is to convict you of sin, and that is what your conscience does.

God gave you a conscience as a way of knowing right from wrong. Your conscience is an inner awareness of what is of God and what is not. It is often accompanied by a sense of peace, a feeling of confirmation, or unease and feeling troubled.

Some people have difficulty hearing because they have ignored their conscience for so long that they have become deaf to it. But, if they put themselves in a position to listen and respond, their ears will open and the whisper of God's still small voice will begin to sound loud and clear.

Here is something to think about

A well-beaten path does not always make the right road.

Cowardice asks the question, is it safe? Expedience asks the question, is it politic? Vanity asks, is it popular? But conscience asks the question, is it right?

There comes a time when one must take a position that is neither safe, nor politic, nor popular, but he must make it because his conscience tells him that it is right. Martin Luther King Jr.

Conscience is what hurts when everything else feels good!

The voice of your conscience is so delicate that it is easy to stifle; but it is also so clear that it is impossible to mistake.

Are you paying attention to your conscience? Is there something you need to do, or to stop doing?

Now is a good time to talk to God about it. You will sleep much better, and you will clear the way for hearing His still small voice.

Chapter 20

Knowing and Growing

G od often speaks to you through the Holy Spirit's promptings. As you train yourself to take more notice when you sense gentle nudges and promptings, you will begin to hear God through subtle impressions and inner knowing.

Hearing God through your intuition

Intuition, impressions and perception are all shades of the same thing. They are some of the many ways that God uses to get your attention and speak to you.

Sometimes you might get a slight impression of something, or you may have a gut feeling; people often refer to this as intuition.

- Intuition is simply the ability to understand something instinctively, without reasoning it out or discovering it. Intuition simply knows something spontaneously.

- **Perception is** the ability to understand or notice something easily, **and it involves being intuitively aware.**
- An impression is very similar - people tend to use the word *impression* when they are referring to a prompting or nudge of the Holy Spirit.

Everyone has intuitive feelings at some level - a gut feeling, or simply knowing something without learning it or being told about it. The New Testament speaks about the disciples perceiving things; God has given you the ability to perceive things too.

Whatever you choose to call it - intuition, perception or an impression, it is simply knowing something without using your natural senses or working it out.

Ask the Holy Spirit to magnify those inner nudges and help you to develop your spiritual senses so that you can be more aware of hidden things, and the thoughts and intentions of other people's hearts.

The more you take notice of these slight impressions, trust the Holy Spirit's promptings, and act on what you perceive, the more sensitive you will become to God's voice.

God *is* speaking to you through subtle impressions. I encourage you to start taking more notice of them. Step out in faith and begin to act on your intuition rather than dismissing it as being your own thoughts and ideas.

When you start paying attention to subtle impressions you will sometimes get it wrong. Please do not let that put you off. *You do not start off being an expert; give yourself permission to be a learner.* If you persevere and allow yourself to learn through your mistakes, you will eventually get it right more of the time.

When you keep on stepping out in faith, your level of spiritual awareness will increase. Have the courage to trust that God is speaking to you through your intuition and act on what you sense.

If you would like reassurance that what you are sensing really is God prompting you, share what you believe you are hearing with a trusted advisor before stepping out and acting on what you believe you hear.

Chapter 21

The Rocks Call Out His Name!

I Hope you are beginning to believe that God really is speaking all the time and that you *can* hear Him. Hearing God is just a matter of learning to recognise the different facets of His voice. He speaks in a variety of ways, including His creation and through natural events.

When you look at the stars, see the sunset, note unusual weather patterns, or experience a storm, if you look with the eyes of your heart, you can see the fingerprints of God.

God's glory is on tour in the skies, God-craft on exhibit across the horizon. Madame Day holds classes every morning, Professor Night lectures each evening. Their words aren't heard, their voices aren't recorded, But their silence fills the earth: unspoken truth is spoken everywhere. Psalm 19:1-4

You will begin to understand more about the spiritual realm once you start noticing things in the natural realm because events in the natural world are a shadow of the spiritual world.

You can hear God by looking at His creation, and you can discover a lot about His ways through events that unfold around you. When unnatural things occur, such as a sudden fog, snow out of season, or a spate of floods, ask the Lord, *"What are you saying to me through this happening, Lord?"*

God is constantly speaking through His physical creation

Ask for eyes to see and begin to take notice of sudden changes in the weather. Ask God to reveal the meaning of unfolding events. If you see something unusual, ask God what He is saying to you through it.

Press in and ask God for understanding of the times and seasons. Ask Him to peel back the curtain and speak to you through nature and current events.

The Spider's Web

We have big wrought iron gates at the end of our driveway. They were left open overnight and the next morning there was a giant spider's web completely filling the opening. It was an amazing sight.

A web is where a spider catches and stores food. Was this a sign that God would provide for us? Or did it signify a web of lies and deceit? As things turned out, it was both.

Seeing that amazing sight helped to show us that God knew what was going to happen beforehand, and that He cared enough to cause us to stop and take notice, and put us on our guard. This warning and promise of provision helped us to respond in faith in the middle of a testing situation.

When events unfolded, we were able to respond with confidence, knowing that God was well aware and would provide all we needed.

If you want to learn more about hearing God in this way, and discover the spiritual meaning behind natural events, I highly recommend that you read, *If This Were A Dream What Would It Mean?* By Murray Dueck.

Chapter 22

Personal Prophecy

In 1 Corinthians 14:1 it says, follow after love, and earnestly desire spiritual gifts, especially that you may prophesy. God gives the gift of prophecy to encourage, exhort, and to bless people. It is one of His ways of speaking directly to you for yourself or for others.

How do you hear prophecy?

Prophecy is a gift. The Bible says it is a gift that you can stir up and fan into flame. You can ask God to give you insight and speak to you about situations and, if it is appropriate, He will.

When receiving prophecy, some people hear words within their spirit. Words that appear as sudden thoughts that cut across what you were thinking. Other people might see an image, or a vision, that speaks into a situation.

I have a friend who sees words written on people's foreheads, and other friends who see words as if they are on a screen. I wish it was always that easy, but it isn't!

The Bible says that we prophesy in part. Sometimes God chooses to show you only part of the picture. In these cases, the message you receive is likely to be symbolic in nature rather than clear and spelled out.

The Bible shows us Jesus teaching people through parables; God still speaks in this way today. You may not always understand the message you hear. It may sometimes seem as though it is not relevant and that you must have heard wrongly. Yet when you are brave enough to step out and deliver the message, the person receiving the prophecy will know exactly what it means, and it will speak directly to their need.

Interpreting prophecy

God always speaks accurately, but you might not always hear Him perfectly. It is easy to take the information that God gives you and come to the wrong conclusion. That does not necessarily mean that the prophecy was wrong, it could simply be that you misunderstood the interpretation.

Unless you are sure that God has given you the interpretation of the message, it is wise to simply deliver what you hear without offering an interpretation.

If you ever give or receive a prophetic word that does not seem accurate, look at the original prophecy, and see if there could be an alternative interpretation.

A word of caution

People have a tendency to hear what they want to hear. Please be aware that you hear through a filter, and be careful that in your enthusiasm you do not read things into prophecy that God has not said.

Prophecy is conditional

Prophecy needs a response. Even when the prophecy does not contain precise instructions, there is usually an implied action. It could be as simple as receiving the word, mixing it with faith and taking action on what you have heard.

All through Scripture, whenever God gives a promise, there is a condition attached. God's promises are often delivered as, "If you do this ...then I will." Fulfilment of prophecy is often conditional on your response to what God says.

Directive prophecy

Directive prophecy will usually confirm what God has already spoken to you, or be confirmed in other ways. I would not recommend acting on directional prophecy until you have confirmation.

Sometimes it is best to put the prophecy on the shelf while you wait for God to show you what to do with it. Some prophetic words are given to prepare you, or to give you vision for what is ahead. Prophecy is not always for immediate action.

You need to judge prophecy according to

Scripture. If it holds true, receive it with faith and pray it into being, yet do remember to be patient and wait for God's timing. When the time is right, God will bring it to pass.

I would like to share a story with you to illustrate what I mean

In the summer of 2006 my life was at a very low ebb. I suffer from nerve damage and muscle weakness and I had come to a point where I was in continual discomfort. Every day was a trial. I struggled to walk, I could not look after my family, and I felt like giving up.

After a day of feeling particularly sorry for myself and crying out for God's help, I felt prompted to take a folder of the shelf. I spent the whole evening reading through the file. There were pieces of journaling and prophetic words spanning 10 years.

As I read, I noted that while many of the things I felt God had spoken to me had actually happened, there were two that I had cherished in my heart for many years that had not yet come to pass.

I noted them in my journal and asked God to show me whether they were just my imagination or whether they really were part of my destiny in Him.

The next day, someone who was prophetically gifted, announced from the front of the church meeting that while preparing for the meeting, the Lord had shown him a picture of someone taking a folder off a shelf containing prophecies that were still to be fulfilled.

He described exactly what I had done the night before and finished by saying, "God wants you to know that the prophecies are from Him and that He wants you to speak life into them."

I approached him at the end of the meeting and told him the events of the night before. He prayed for me, and I declared that God's word was true, and spoke life into the prophecies as directed.

Three months later, I started my Closer Walk With God blog and a few months later I began creating my Christian Life Coaching website. I am writing books and creating audios, I am training people to be Christian Life Coaches and I love what I am doing. The Lord is fulfilling the words that He spoke to me and opening up doors I could not even imagine back then.

And though I still struggle physically, I know that God has spoken and I am confident that there is more to come. I encourage myself with the knowledge that God will complete the work that He has begun, and when circumstances suggest otherwise, I remind myself of God's words and speak His word to the circumstances.

Once you have heard God speak, it is easier to press on in faith regardless of the circumstances you find yourself in. When you receive a prophetic word and mix it with faith, you can step out in full assurance that God will do what He has promised. Sometimes you need to battle to see the word come to pass. God's command is, *"Believe and do not doubt. Only believe!"*

Chapter 23

God Still Speaks Through Dreams

From the beginning of time God has spoken to people through dreams. There are examples all the way though the Bible. God still speaks through dreams today, and He uses dreams to accomplish many things.

Dreams...

- Bring counsel; the Lord can use your dreams to counsel you and show you what to do.
- Sometimes lead to emotional healing.
- Bring direction; sometimes you know exactly what to do next as the result of a dream.
- Sometimes bring instruction from God.
- On occasions reveal something you need to know.
- Inspire and encourage.
- Are sometimes used by God to make you aware of His plans and intentions.

So why does God sometimes use dreams to communicate with you rather than speak directly to you?

Dreams bypass your conscious mind which often gets in the way of you hearing. God sometimes speaks through dreams as a way of getting past your natural defences and resistance.

Eight things to bear in mind

1. **Your dream is likely to be about you and for you**. 95% of the dreams you dream are likely to be about you and your life rather than about someone else.

2. **Most dreams are symbolic.** Train yourself to look at your dreams symbolically. Dreams are rarely literal. The meaning may be personal to you. Ask yourself, "What does this represent to me?" When you are trying to understand what God is saying in the dream, look for metaphors and similes that will help you to unravel the meaning.

3. **Your dreams often deal with concerns that you are facing now.** Ask, "What issues were concerning me when I had the dream?" When you know what you were thinking about before you had the dream, it is often much easier to understand your dream.

4. **Ask the Holy Spirit to help you** to understand what your dream is speaking into, and to make the interpretation obvious to you.

5. **When you reach the correct interpretation, you will know**. If you sense that your conclusions do not "feel quite right," you have probably not arrived at the true interpretation yet.

6. **Dreams will often help you see things that you have been blind to.** But please note that God does not give you dreams to condemn you, it is simply His way of drawing your attention to something.

7. **Ask, "What is the purpose of this dream**? Why did God give me this dream and cause me to remember it?"

8. **Never make a major decision based only on a dream.** Look for confirmation through the many different ways that God speaks to you. Peace in your heart, the counsel of others, God's Word, His still small voice, prophecy...

You will find it helps if you train yourself to think outside the box. God will often use unexpected ways to get your attention and speak to you. Look for clever wordplay and learn to think laterally.

The easiest way to interpret a dream is to identify the main elements first. Start with the first symbol and try to interpret it. Do the same with the next symbol. Continually ask yourself, "What does this represent to me?"

Once you know what the symbolic pictures mean, retrace your steps through the dream seeking revelation until you sense that you know what God is saying to you.

I recommend that you start recording your dreams and set time aside to seek God for their meaning.

If you would like more help to understand the dreams that God has caused you to dream, you will find an audio recording in the bonus resources.

Streams Ministries offers outstanding courses that train you how to understand your dreams and how to help other people to decode the messages that God is communicating as they sleep. To learn more, go to streamsministries.org

Chapter 24

Don't Panic!

What do you do when you are struggling to hear God and He seems far away? I have experienced days, weeks, and even months when I did not seem to be able to hear what God was saying about matters that were important to me. Yet looking back, I can see that although God seemed silent at the time, He was actively working in my life. God is always at work and He is always speaking; it is simply that He does not always tell you what He is doing and why.

When God seems strangely silent about something, remember that He *is* faithful, and trust that you *will* hear Him when the time is right.

How Do You Respond When God Seems Silent?

It can be discouraging when God seems to be silent about things that are dear to your heart. It is often easier to go through things when you know why they are happening, but God does not always let you in on the why.

So what do you do when the enemy tries to tell you lies like these?

- What makes you think that you can hear God?
- God isn't going to speak to you, you don't deserve it.
- You don't really know God at all.
- God doesn't care about you.
- He's given up on you.
- God doesn't speak to people today, you've just been making it all up.

You have a choice. You can rely on your feelings, or you can continue to trust God's Word and His promises.

When God seems strangely silent

- Hold on to what you already know – what is the last thing God said to you?
- Consider that God could be testing you – what do you *really* believe?
- Decide that you will not start to doubt what you know.
- Resist comparing yourself to other people.
- Beware of making things more complicated than they are – faith is childlike.
- Make your mind up to walk by faith rather than by sight.

God promised that He would never leave you or forsake you. God is always with you whether you are aware of it or not, whether you can hear Him easily or not. When God seems silent, look for His guidance even in the apparent silence. Remember, and continue to believe that

- God has guided you in the past.
- He is guiding you now.
- He will guide you in the future.

God's apparent silence is an invitation to take your eyes off the circumstances and fix your eyes on Jesus who is the Author and Finisher of your faith. Dare to trust God and draw even closer.

Chapter 25

Removing the Obstacles

There are many reasons why you might struggle to hear God speaking. If you are finding it hard to hear God, give yourself a spiritual check-up and clear away any obstacles there might be so that you can hear God more clearly. It will be much easier to hear God once you identify the obstacles and clear them out of the way.

Possible obstacles to hearing God

Thinking that what you hear is your imagination

One of the biggest obstacles to hearing God is thinking that what you hear is just your own thoughts. Scepticism can easily cause you to reject what you hear from the Holy Spirit. The enemy wants you to doubt that God is speaking to you; he wants you to believe that it is just your imagination because he knows that your life will be transformed when you hear God. He goes to great lengths to keep you from your birth-right.

Over-dependence on others to hear God for you

God longs to have a close relationship with *you*. He wants you to hear Him even more than you want to hear Him. Expect to hear God, put yourself into a position where you can easily hear Him, and dare to believe that He really will speak to you.

Being too busy

You will find it easier to hear God when you slow down and create space in your life. Take time to be still enough to deliberately listen for God's voice, and train yourself to recognise when it is God speaking rather than your own thoughts.

Turn down the noise and turn up the volume!

God often speaks quietly. Elijah recognised that God was speaking in a whisper rather than in the raging wind, earthquake or fire. Turn down the noise; be ruthless in tuning out everything that interferes with you hearing God clearly.

Create favourable circumstances

Give God more opportunities to make Himself heard, create an atmosphere that makes it easy to hear God anytime and anywhere.

Make sure you act on what God says to you

Have you acted on what God has *already* told you? God is looking for followers. He is looking for faith and obedience. Are you ready to lay down your own will and agenda and sincerely ask God what He wants?

If you want to keep on hearing God, make sure that you are willing to act on what He says to you. It is much easier to hear when you receive with faith and are ready to receive and act on what He has to say to you.

Do not expect to hear God if you are walking in disobedience

You need to make sure that you pay attention to the things God reveals. If you have heard God in the past and have not acted on what you heard, you need to put that right with God and let Him know that you are ready to hear, and willing to do whatever He says.

There are many reasons why you might find it hard to hear God.

Have you got a good connection?

Sin, wrong attitudes and unforgiveness can block communication with God. So can greed, selfish ambition, pride, and holding on to your own agenda. God can and does break through the sin barrier – He is God He can do anything! Adam and Eve were still able to hear God even though they had sinned - but when you do not deal with sin, it can get in the way and be an obstacle to hearing from God.

So make sure you are tuned to the right frequency and that there is nothing in the way of you having a good connection, and good reception.

Selective hearing can keep you from hearing God

You might miss a lot of what God is saying if you think He always speaks in particular ways. When God does not speak in the way that you expect, you might not recognize that it is God speaking to you.

You need to be open to God speaking in any way He chooses. Beware of sifting out what you do not want to hear because it is not comfortable or it does not fit with your plans.

What is your motivation for hearing God?

If you are seeking to hear God for selfish reasons and looking to profit from what you hear, or if you are simply looking to achieve your own ambitions – God is unlikely to co-operate no matter how long you pray or fast.

Are you resentful?

Are you angry that God does not seem to be giving you what you want or doing things the way you want Him to? It is easy to slip into thinking that you know best and be scandalised that God does not co-operate with you and do things your way. Resentment will make you deaf to God's voice.

Are you impatient?

Are you in a rush to hear from God about something and not prepared to wait for His timing? I wonder how many times you have missed hearing God speak by giving up just as you were about to break through? Do you want to hear God enough to wait and listen, believing that He will speak?

Are you hungry to hear God?

Proverbs 2:3-5 makes it clear that you need to want to hear God so much that you are prepared to make it a priority and not take no for an answer. It says to make insight a priority, and search for it like you would for treasure. Turn your ear to wisdom, apply your heart to understanding; call out for discernment, and then you will learn what it is to fear God, and find the knowledge of God.

If you have given yourself a spiritual check-up, and put things right with God, you *will* hear God speak when you position yourself to hear. That is God's promise to you.

Ask God to speak to you and wait for His answer. Be like Habakkuk: Stand at your guard post, keep *WATCH* and look out to *SEE* what He will *SPEAK* to you. Habakkuk 2:1-2

How To Respond When You Hear God

One of the tests of spiritual maturity is how you respond when God speaks to you. Whether you hear a still small voice while you are quiet before God, get an impression while reading Scripture, sense the prompting of the Holy Spirit while you are listening to teaching, or receive a personal prophecy, *it is what you do with what you hear that determines the outcome.*

Weigh what you hear, look for confirmation, and if you are sure that God has spoken, take what you hear to God in prayer, ask Him for details and battle for its fulfilment.

Make sure that you combine hearing with faith and action so that you do not lose your prize

Remember that God's timing is not always your timing. Do not be in a hurry to bring things about in your own strength before their proper time. Press in and ask God to reveal the next steps to you.

May you be blessed with a listening heart and hearing ears, may you have an ever increasing sense of God's presence with you, and may you learn to recognize the voice of the lover of your soul.

To help you on your journey, I have gathered extra helps and free online tutorials, you will find them here:

HowToHearGod.co/resources

Be blessed to be a blessing

Meet The Author

Lynne Lee is an experienced Christian Life Coach, Breakthrough Life Coach Trainer, and spiritual mentor. She has over 35 years experience in pastoral care, discipleship and teaching. She has spent all her adult life working with adults and children to help them grow in God and transform their lives.

Her heart's desire is to encourage and equip people just like you to have a closer walk with the Father, and to be led by the Holy Spirit into the life and discipleship of Jesus.

Lynne is married to Timothy Lee. They married after knowing each other for just 18 weeks and went on to have 5 children: Emma, Freddie, Charlie, Katie and Barney. They are based at Community Church Derby where they live in the UK.

Lynne has written many articles on Spiritual and life coaching topics

In 2006, the Lord led Lynne to share some of her accumulated content on the web. As a result she launched her Closer Walk With God blog, and created her Christian Life Coaching website.

Lynne is a Life Coach Trainer

More recently Lynne has trained pastors, small group leaders, teachers, counselors, stay at home mums, business people, psychologists, and life coaches who have trained with secular coaching schools, how to coach people to breakthrough from a Christian perspective.

If you would like to know more about Christian life coaching, or you are thinking of training to be a life coach and would prefer coach training that is based on sound Biblical principles, please visit www.ChristianLifeCoaching.co.uk where you will find a wealth of information to help you on your way.

You can easily connect with Lynne here

Facebook.com/BiblicalLifeCoaching

linkedin.com/in/LynneLee

plus.google.com/+LynneLee

May I Ask A Favour?

May I ask you a favour? I would love for you to leave a review on my Amazon page as your comments will help others looking for help with hearing God, and will assist me in the development of future books.

Thank you so very much.

Be blessed to be a blessing!

Lynne

If you have an Amazon account, sign in as usual. In the Amazon Search box at the top enter *How To Hear God Lynne Lee* to go to my book's listing and follow the instructions for writing a review below.

To write a review

- Click on the title
- Scroll down a bit and you'll see a graph on the left with "Write a customer review" to its right.
- Click the yellow box to write a review.
- Click the on the stars to rate the book (1 star to 5 stars)

- Write a short headline for your review in the Headline box.
- Write your review (20 words minimum).
- Click submit and you will immediately get a "Thanks" message and a follow-up email when your review is published.

If you don't have an Amazon account, you can create one by doing the following (no cost to you):

Go to www.amazon.co.uk or www.amazon.com

Click the drop down menu upper right, "Hello. Sign In Your Account. Choose "New customer? Start here." Register to create a new account with name, email (twice), and make up a password.

In the Amazon Search box at the top enter *How To Hear God Lynne Lee* to go to my book's listing and follow the instructions for writing a review.

Thank you for helping me with your review. Each review is vitally important to the book's success. If you'd like to contact me you can easily message me here:

www.christiancoachingsolutions.com/contact

Recommended Resources

How To Fulfil Your Life Purpose

Practical strategies to help you discover your destiny and fulfil your life purpose – **free** audio training available to download immediately.

bit.ly/1gjr6q6

Life Breakthrough Coaching Training Program

Christian life coach training for people who want to train as a life coach with an experienced trainer who approaches life coaching from a Biblical perspective. If you are a mentor, pastor, lay leader, counselor or life coach and you want to add Biblical life coaching skills to your business or ministry then this effective yet affordable Life Breakthrough Coach Training is for you.

bit.ly/1qDszAu

Student testimonial

"I knew that coaching was about getting from where you are to where you want to be. What I didn't know was that this course would take me from a place of very little knowledge about coaching to a whole new world of breakthrough for myself and others!!

I loved this course and I love coaching!! I especially love the way that as a result God is beginning to use me to partner with Him to see lives transformed. It is so powerful!

While I will be always growing as a coach, this course has been an inspirational foundation and launch pad to give me a flying start! I cannot believe how much we have covered in 10 weeks but I have felt supported every step of the way. Although fast paced it is an exciting and exhilarating journey! It has left me feeling passionate about developing into the best coach that I can be and I am very grateful!!

Andrea Tibbits

Recommended Books

Spirit Talk ~ Larry Randolph

The Pursuit Of God ~ AW Tozer

The Practice of the Presence of God ~ Brother Lawrence

If This Were A Dream, What Would It Mean? ~ Murray Dueck

Websites With Helpful Resources

StreamsMinistries.com

CwgMinistries.org

CPSIA information can be obtained at www.ICGtesting.com
Printed in the USA
LVOW06s1539100414

381195LV00004B/404/P